Lady Bird Johnson

MW01268756

Lady Bird Johnson

Making Our Neighborhoods Beautiful

by Charnan Simon

Children's Press®
A Division of Grolier Publishing
New York London Hong Kong Sydney
Danbury, Connecticut

Photo Credits

Photographs ©: AP/Wide World Photos: 2; Archive Photos: 37 left; Brown Brothers: 15, 25; Christianson/Leberman, Austin, TX: 18; Comstock: 7; Corbis-Bettmann: 3; Envision: 44 (Jean Higgins); Gamma-Liaison: 33 (Yvonne Hemsey), cover, 43 (Zigy Kaluzny); Jay Mallin Photos: back cover, 31, 38 (Jay Mallin), 32 (Paul Page); LBJ Library Collection: 8 (Robert Knudsen), 23 (Cecil Stoughton), 11, 12, 13, 29; Photo Researchers: 45 (Linda Bartlett), 36 (David R. Frazier), 41 (Adam Jones); Tom Kazunas: 48; UPI/Corbis-Bettmann: 10, 17, 19, 21, 27, 35, 37 right, 40.

Reading Consultant
Linda Cornwell, Learning Resource Consultant
Indiana Department of Education

Visit Children's Press on the Internet at:
http://publishing.grolier.com

Library of Congress Cataloging-in-Publication Data

Simon, Charnan.
    Lady Bird Johnson : making our neighborhoods beautiful / by Charnan Simon.
        p. cm. — (Community builders)
    Includes index.
    Summary: A simple biography of former First Lady Lady Bird Johnson, focusing on her efforts to beautify the nation.
    ISBN: 0-516-20292-8 (lib. bdg.)   0-516-26134-7 (pbk.)
    1. Johnson, Lady Bird, 1912-   —Juvenile literature. 2. Presidents' spouses—United States—Biography—Juvenile literature. 3. Urban beautification—United States—Juvenile literature. 4. Roadside improvement—United States—Juvenile literature. [1. Johnson, Lady Bird, 1912-   . 2. First ladies.] I. Title. II. Series: Simon, Charnan. Community builders.
E848.J64S56 1997
973.923'092—dc20
[B]   96-36148
                                                   CIP
                                                     AC

Contents

Chapter ONE

This Land Is Your Land

Have you ever sung the song "America the Beautiful"? Have you ever thought about how beautiful our country really is? We have mountains and meadows, forests and fields. We have many impressive buildings in our cities. We have flowers and trees in our parks.

But our country can't stay beautiful by itself. Each of us has to do our part to keep the United States looking its best.

Many American cities have tried to preserve
their natural surroundings.

Lady Bird and Lyndon Johnson together in the White House during Lyndon's presidency

One person who has worked hard to beautify America is a woman named Lady Bird Johnson. Lady Bird is an environmentalist. Today Lady Bird lives in Austin, the capital of Texas. But for many years, she lived in our nation's capital, Washington, D.C. Her husband, Lyndon B. Johnson, was the thirty-fifth president of the United States.

As First Lady, Lady Bird worked hard to protect our country's natural beauty. She planted trees and flowers and shrubs across America. She encouraged everyone she met to do the same. She even got laws passed to make sure America stayed beautiful.

One of the most important things Lady Bird did was to bring wildflowers back to America. Have you ever taken a ride into the country and seen wild-flowers? Once our country was filled with them. No one planted them—they just grew wild in meadows and by streams. Today, buildings and roads have been built where many of these flowers once blossomed. Instead of meadows, there are highways and parking lots.

Lady Bird Johnson wanted to change this. She loved seeing wildflowers waving in the wind. She

Environmentalists

People who work to protect the land and other resources, such as trees and water, are called environmentalists. Environmentalists want to conserve our country's natural beauty.

Lady Bird traveled across the United States as part of her efforts to help people appreciate nature. Here, she visits the Santa Fe National Forest in Santa Fe, New Mexico.

wanted everyone to have a chance to enjoy these native blossoms. So she started the National Wildflower Research Center near her home in Austin, Texas. This center has helped to bring the beauty of wildflowers back to America.

Lady Bird Johnson has dedicated her life to helping to make our country more beautiful. This is the story of how she did it.

"Pretty as a Ladybird"

Lady Bird Johnson was born in the little town of Karnack, Texas, on December 22, 1912. She was named Claudia Alta Taylor, but no one called her by her real name. When she was just a baby, a nursemaid said, "Why, she's as pretty as a ladybird!" From then on, everyone called her Lady Bird.

Lady Bird and
her nanny in 1913

As a child, Lady Bird enjoyed her country lifestyle.

When Lady Bird was just five years old, her mother died. Lady Bird's Aunt Effie came to help take care of her. Aunt Effie loved books, music, and nature. She taught Lady Bird to do the same. "She opened my spirit to beauty," Lady Bird once said about her aunt.

As a child, Lady Bird was shy. She lived out in the country. She went to a one-room school. There were not many children for her to play with, but Lady Bird was not lonely. "I was a child of nature," she explains. "My life consisted of roaming the hills, creeks, and woods."

Lady Bird especially loved watching the flowers burst into color in spring. When the first daffodil bloomed, she would have her own little ceremony and crown it queen of all the flowers.

Lady Bird may have been shy, but she had a sense of adventure. When she grew older, she studied journalism (writing for newspapers) at the University of Texas. She thought "people in the press went more places and met more interesting people and had more exciting things happen to them."

Lady Bird was just twenty-one years old when she met a young man named Lyndon Johnson. Lyndon was tall and smart and energetic. The minute he met Lady Bird, he knew she was the girl for him. He asked her to marry him on their very first date! Two

Lyndon and Lady Bird during their honeymoon in Mexico

The U.S. Congress

The United States Congress is the legislative branch of our government. It is the branch where the country's laws are made. Congress is divided into two parts—the House of Representatives and the Senate. Members of Congress are elected by the people who live in their same district or state.

months later, on November 17, 1934, Lyndon and Lady Bird were married.

Lyndon was an ambitious young man. He had been the secretary to a congressman in Washington, D.C. Now he wanted to serve in the United States Congress himself.

In 1937, Lyndon won his first congressional election. Now Lady Bird would be the wife of a member of the House of Representatives.

The next years were busy ones for Lady Bird. She helped Lyndon answer mail and write speeches. She

Lady Bird in the 1930s

took visitors on tours of the nation's capital. She entertained Lyndon's many friends and political partners.

When the United States entered World War II in 1941, Lady Bird became even busier. Lyndon had to leave Washington in 1942 to serve in the U.S. Navy. While he was away, Lady Bird worked full-time, running his congressional office.

Texas

Texas is our country's second-largest state. Its capital city is Austin, which is located near the center of the state.

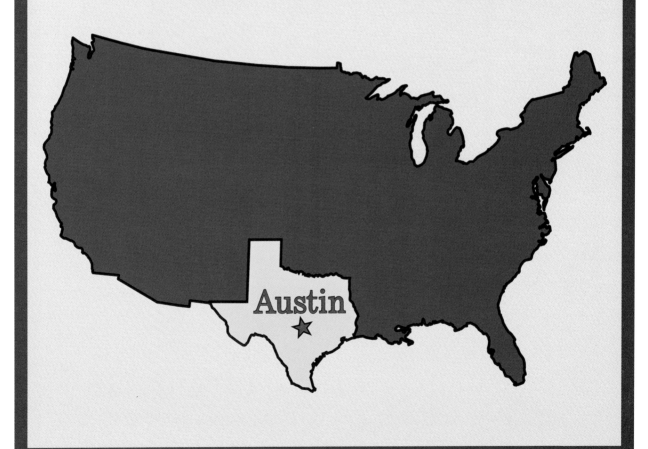

Lyndon served in the navy after the Japanese bombing of Pearl Harbor, Hawaii, on December 7, 1941.

Even though Lady Bird was living in Washington, D.C., she didn't forget her Texas roots. In 1942, she used money she had inherited from her mother to buy a radio station in Austin, Texas. When Lady Bird ⬚⬚⬚⬚ tion, it was ⬚⬚⬚⬚ Lady Bird d⬚⬚⬚⬚thing about ⬚⬚⬚ station. But she was a quick learner and a hard worker. Soon her station was making money. With Lady Bird in charge, the station grew into a successful business.

By 1944, Lyndon was back in Washington. That was the year the Johnsons' first daughter, Lynda Bird, was born. Their second daughter, Luci Baines, followed three

Lady Bird and the Johnsons' two daughters, Luci Baines (middle) and Lynda Bird (right)

years later. Now Lady Bird was a congressman's wife, a successful businesswoman, and a busy mother of two little girls. She divided her time between the Johnsons' Washington, D.C., home and their beautiful new Texas ranch.

In 1948, Lyndon ran for the U.S. Senate. Being a senator would be an advancement for him. Senators serve six years in Congress. Members of the House serve only two years. This was an important election for Lyndon. He needed Lady Bird's help.

Lady Bird was still very shy. It was hard for her to speak in public. But when Lady Bird made up her mind to do something, she did it! She actively began campaigning with her husband. Instead of just smiling and waving while Lyndon gave speeches, Lady Bird starting giving speeches herself. Her hard

18

work paid off when Lyndon won the election!

In 1954, Lyndon Johnson ran for reelection to the Senate. This time, Lady Bird decided to do even more to help her husband. "I got real annoyed with myself for being so shy and quiet," she said, "and never having anything to say when asked to speak." So she took a series of speech lessons. "It turned out to be one of the most delightful, expanding experiences I've ever had," she said proudly.

Once again, Lyndon won his election. But just a year later, in 1955, he had a heart attack. Lady Bird promptly moved into the hospital room next to her husband's. While he rested and got well, she ran his office for him. Her husband was only half-joking when he said that voters would happily have elected her instead of him.

Lady Bird overcame her shyness to be an active campaigner for her husband.

Chapter THREE

Early White House Years

In 1960, Lyndon Johnson ran as vice president with presidential candidate John F. Kennedy. Lady Bird threw herself into the campaign. She traveled more than 35,000 miles (56,000 kilometers), giving speeches and shaking hands. She wanted to make sure Lyndon didn't give himself another heart attack by working too hard.

When John Kennedy won the election, Lyndon Johnson became vice president of the United States. As the vice president's wife, Lady Bird was busier than ever. She helped Mrs. Kennedy entertain large groups of people. She spoke to women's

Lady Bird in the gown she wore for her husband's
inauguration as vice president on January 20, 1961

Goodwill Ambassador

A goodwill ambassador is someone who unofficially represents her government in foreign countries. She tries to make a good impression by being caring and friendly. This helps the people of other countries want to work together with her own country.

organizations throughout the country. With her husband, she traveled to thirty-three countries around the world as a goodwill ambassador.

Then tragedy struck. On November 22, 1963, President John F. Kennedy was shot and killed while he was visiting Dallas, Texas. Vice President Lyndon B. Johnson became the new president, and in an instant, Lady Bird Johnson's life changed. Now that her husband was president, she was First Lady of the United States.

Lyndon Johnson was sworn in as president following President Kennedy's assassination. Looking on are Lady Bird (left of Lyndon) and Jacqueline Kennedy (right), wife of the slain president.

By early December, the Johnson family was settled in the White House. Lyndon reassured Americans that their government would continue to run smoothly, despite President Kennedy's death. As always, Lady Bird worked right alongside her husband.

A big part of any First Lady's job is entertaining important people from around the world. While the Johnsons were in the White House, they entertained more than 200,000 guests! Lady Bird tried to learn something about each of her guests before they arrived. This helped her talk to them about their interests, their countries, even their families. She wanted her guests to feel comfortable and to enjoy themselves in her home. Everyone agreed that Lady Bird was a warm and gracious hostess.

Lady Bird also liked to host "Women Do-ers" luncheons. She invited women from all professions to these luncheons. Together, they discussed many important issues. They talked about the arts, poverty, women's rights, children, crime, and foreign affairs. Then they talked about what they could do to make the world a better place.

Lady Bird often felt that women were ignored by the government. She thought this was not only wrong, it was foolish. Women had so much to offer, it was just silly not to use their talents. Lady Bird urged Lyndon to give women important government

As First Lady, Lady Bird enjoyed discussing
important topics with other women, and sharing
ideas for improving life for everyone.

jobs. And at the end of the day, Lady Bird often asked, "Well, what did you do for women today?"

Lady Bird was also very active in some of her husband's official programs. One of President Johnson's most important programs was his "War on Poverty." This was a group of laws and plans that helped underprivileged Americans. Lady Bird found one program, called Head Start, especially interesting. Head Start made sure that young children had proper food and medical care. It helped them learn about reading and math so they would be ready to start school. Lady Bird became Head Start's national chairperson. She traveled all over the country to help Head Start succeed.

Lady Bird was also an active supporter of the Civil Rights Act of 1964, which President Johnson signed into law on July 2, 1964. The Civil Rights Act declared that all Americans, no matter what color they were, could go to the same schools, work at the same jobs, and sleep in the same hotels. And all Americans could play in the same parks and eat in the same restaurants.

**As the national chairperson for Head Start,
Lady Bird traveled throughout the country
and met children taking part in the program.**

Before the Civil Rights Act was passed, many states—especially those in the South—had segregation laws. These laws kept black Americans and white Americans separate. Even after the Civil Rights Act was passed, some people still believed in

27

segregation. Many of these people were angry with the president for signing the Civil Rights Act.

Soon after the Act passed, Lyndon Johnson began campaigning for a full term as president. Lady Bird began campaigning, too. But this time she didn't just go places with Lyndon. She campaigned all by herself, something only one other First Lady, Eleanor Roosevelt, had ever done.

Lady Bird rode on a special train called the *Lady Bird Special* through eight southern states.

Eleanor Roosevelt

Eleanor Roosevelt was the wife of Franklin D. Roosevelt, who was president from 1933 to 1945. Eleanor was an active First Lady. She traveled widely and spoke out on a number of important issues. Lady Bird Johnson is often compared to Eleanor Roosevelt.

Lady Bird
(at podium)
campaigning
from the train
she rode
through the
southern states

Whenever the train stopped, Lady Bird stepped onto a platform on the caboose and spoke to the crowd.

Some of the southerners who were angry with Lyndon Johnson because of the Civil Rights Act might not have listened to him speak. But they listened to Lady Bird. She defended her husband and his beliefs about equal rights. She gave forty-seven speeches in four days. The shy little girl from Karnack, Texas, had come a long way!

"She Planted a Tree"

Lyndon Johnson won the November 1964 presidential election. After the campaign, Lady Bird started working on her own special project.

Ever since she was a little girl, Lady Bird had loved nature. As First Lady, she started a program to preserve America's natural beauty for everyone to enjoy.

Lady Bird began right in Washington, D.C. She created the First Lady's Committee for a More

Lady Bird believed that if people had a chance
to appreciate nature, they would be more willing
to preserve its beauty.

When Lady Bird decided to start her beautification
project, she began in Washington, D.C., by creating the
First Lady's Committee for a More Beautiful Capital.

Beautiful Capital. She encouraged neighborhoods to clean up their parks, streets, and school yards. She asked everyone to help her plant trees, shrubs, and flowers. Lady Bird herself helped to plant more than two million daffodils in Washington!

Everywhere she went, Lady Bird talked about the connection between ugliness and crime. She believed that people would be happier if they were

Lady Bird believed that people, especially those in inner-city areas, would feel better if their neighborhoods were more beautiful.

Urban Renewal

Helping people clean up and improve their cities is called "urban renewal." Lady Bird Johnson was a pioneer in urban renewal. She urged people in cities everywhere to take pride in their communities.

surrounded by beauty. Happy people were more likely to think good thoughts and do good deeds. But being surrounded by ugliness could make people mean and unhappy. Lady Bird wanted to improve the quality of people's lives by surrounding them with beauty.

Lady Bird didn't stop in Washington, D.C. She found areas that needed cleaning up all over the country. She traveled more than 200,000 miles (322,000 km) to help people make the places where they lived more beautiful. She climbed mountains. She rafted down rivers. She hiked through mead-

Lady Bird traveled extensively as part of her campaign to keep America beautiful. Here, she relaxes beside Jackson Lake in Wyoming.

ows and forests. Everywhere she went, Lady Bird urged people to protect the land and its natural resources. She asked all Americans to join her in planting a tree, a bush, or a shrub to help make our country more beautiful.

Scenes such as this one along a highway in San Antonio, Texas, disappointed Lady Bird.

One thing bothered Lady Bird as she traveled across the United States. Advertising billboards lined the nation's highways. Instead of seeing beautiful scenery as they drove along, motorists saw ugly signs. So Lady Bird went to Congress. She argued that the billboards should be taken down. Instead of signs, motorists should see fields of wildflowers.

Congress listened to Lady Bird. In October 1965, Congress passed a bill to protect the natural environment and beautify the nation's highways. Officially, this bill was called the Highway Beautification Act. Unofficially, it was known as Lady Bird's Bill.

Lady Bird continued her work. She sponsored a White House Conference on Natural Beauty. She gave many more speeches. She asked businesses to donate money to city parks and gardens. She urged citizens to support the National Park Service. And everywhere she went, she planted more trees, flowers, and bushes. She said that when she died, all she wanted people to say about her was, "She planted a tree."

Above: President Johnson hands Lady Bird the pen he used to sign the Highway Beautification Act.

Left: Lady Bird planted many trees and flowers while encouraging others to do the same.

Riders enjoy the daffodils in Lady Bird
Johnson Park in Washington, D.C.

Chapter FIVE

Home to Texas

Lady Bird and Lyndon Johnson left Washington, D.C., in 1969. Lady Bird had enjoyed her five years as First Lady, but she was happy to return to their beloved ranch in Austin, Texas.

The people in Washington were sorry to see Lady Bird go. They were grateful for all she had done to make their city a better place to live. To thank her, they named a park blooming with dogwood trees and hundreds of flowers Lady Bird Johnson Park.

Lady Bird spent her first year in Texas writing a book about her years as First Lady. *A White House Diary* was published in 1970. It tells all about Lady Bird's busy and exciting years in the White House.

In 1973, Lyndon Johnson died. Lady Bird had been married to Lyndon for nearly forty years. She missed him terribly when he died. But she had her daughters and grandchildren to help comfort her. And she had her work to keep her busy.

Lady Bird was still a very busy woman. Her radio station in Austin had turned into a big business. She also worked to raise money for the Lyndon B. Johnson Library and Museum in Austin. She helped run the University of Texas by serving on its board of regents. And she worked for favorite organizations

Lady Bird sits in a patch of wildflowers at the National Wildflower Research Center in Stonewall, Texas.

Bluebonnets bring striking color to a hillside
in Lady Bird's beloved Texas.

such as the National Park Service and the American
Conservation Association.

But the project nearest Lady Bird's heart is the
National Wildflower Research Center. Lady
Bird founded this center in 1982. She donated
$125,000 and 60 acres (24 hectares) of her own
land to start the center. Her goal was to preserve
the native flora—the flowers, grasses, and trees—
of America.

Today more than five hundred species of native
plants flourish in the Wildflower Center. It is

the only center in the nation devoted entirely to native plants and flowers. Gardeners and botanists from all over the country use the center to learn about wildflowers.

Lady Bird got the idea for the center when she and Lyndon moved back to Texas in 1969. She was dismayed by what she saw as they drove through her home state. "The meadows and hillsides were all being replaced by highways and shopping malls. I wanted to try to restore some of our native habitat."

Today if you drive through Texas, you will see wildflowers as well as shopping malls. Texas is especially beautiful in the spring. That is when acres of flowers paint the fields and roadsides. You can see Texas bluebonnets, pink evening primroses, purple horsemint, Indian blankets, and black-eyed Susans.

Lady Bird Johnson has done many things to be proud of in her life. But she is most proud of the National Wildflower Research Center. As she says, "If I can get people to see the beauty of the native flora of their own corner of the world with caring eyes, then I'll be real happy."

Lady Bird Johnson continues her work to
help people appreciate the beauty of nature.

In Your Community

Lady Bird Johnson has devoted much of her life to making America beautiful. What can you do to help?
- Can you help keep your neighborhood park clean or pick up trash along your sidewalk?
- Can you start a wild-flower garden? Your local

Timeline

1912 — Claudia Alta (Lady Bird) Taylor is born on December 22 in Karnack, Texas.

Lady Bird graduates from the University of Texas. — **1933**

1934 — Lady Bird and Lyndon Johnson are married on November 17.

Lady Bird helps Lyndon win his first congressional campaign. — **1937**

1942 — Lady Bird takes over Lyndon's congressional office while he serves in the navy.

Lady Bird buys radio station KTBC in Austin, Texas. — **1942**

1944 — Lynda Bird Johnson is born on March 19.

Luci Baines Johnson is born on July 2. — **1947**

1948 — Lyndon Johnson is elected to the U.S. Senate.

Lyndon Johnson is elected vice president of the United States. — **1960**

nursery can help you pick the right flowers to plant.

• Can you visit one of our national parks and learn how they are helping to preserve America's beauty? Ask your parents if this would make a good family vacation.

• Are there any walking paths or bicycle trails near your home? Lady Bird wanted people to get out and enjoy nature. Take your family for a Sunday afternoon hike or ride!

1963

Lyndon Johnson is elected as president; Lady Bird's train tour through the South is critical to his successful campaign.

John F. Kennedy is assassinated on November 22; Lyndon Johnson becomes president; Lady Bird becomes First Lady.

1964

1965

The Highway Beautification Act (Lady Bird's Bill) is passed by Congress in October.

1968

Lyndon Johnson does not seek reelection as president.

1969

Lady Bird and Lyndon move back to their Texas ranch.

1970

Lady Bird publishes *A White House Diary.*

1973

Lyndon Johnson dies of a heart attack on January 22.

1982

Lady Bird starts the National Wildflower Research Center near Austin, Texas.

1995

The National Wildflower Research Center opens its new, expanded site.

To Find Out More

Here are some additional resources to help you learn more about Lady Bird Johnson, the National Wildflower Research Center, and more:

Books

Anthony, Carl Sferrazza. *America's Most Influential First Ladies.* The Oliver Press, 1992.

Clinton, Susan. *First Ladies.* Children's Press, 1994.

Forey, Pam. *Wild Flowers.* Thunder Bay Press, 1994.

Fradin, Dennis Brindell. *Texas.* Children's Press, 1992.

Horwitz, Margot. *Claudia "Lady Bird" Taylor Johnson.* (Encyclopedia of First Ladies). Children's Press, 1998.

Mayo, Edith P. (ed.). *The Smithsonian Book of the First Ladies.* Henry Holt, 1996.

Organizations and Online Sites

The National Wildflower Research Center
4801 La Cross Avenue
Austin, TX 78739
http://www.Instar.com/mall/ wildflower

National Head Start Association
201 N. Union Street, Suite 320
Alexandria, VA 22314
http://www.nhsa.org/

National Parks and Conservation Association
1776 Massachusetts Avenue N.W.
Suite 200
Washington, D.C. 20036

The First Ladies
http://www2.whitehouse.gov/ WH/glimpse/firstladies/html/ firstladies.html
Full-page biography of each first lady, including a portrait and links to other sites.

Index

About the Author

Charnan Simon lives in Madison, Wisconsin, with her husband and her two daughters. She is a former editor at *Cricket* magazine and has written many books for young people, including Community Builders biographies of Andrew Carnegie, Jane Addams, Jesse Jackson, and others.

Ms. Simon is lucky to be able to write her books while looking out at a woodland wildflower garden filled with white trillium, mayapples, Virginia bluebells, wild ginger, meadow rue, Dutchman's-breeches, jack-in-the-pulpit, dogtooth violets, wild geraniums, bloodroot, Jacob's ladder, wake-robin, bleeding heart, Solomon's seal, wild columbine, and one shooting star.